Book 1
Body Butters For Beginners
BY LINDSEY P

&

Book 2

Soap Making For Beginners
BY LINDSEY P

Book 1
Body Butters For Beginners
BY LINDSEY P

Proven Secrets To Making All Natural Body Butters For Rejuvenating And Hydrating Your Skin

Table Of Contents

Introduction... 5

Chapter 1 Deeper Than Skin Deep.. 6

Chapter 2 Which Is Which? 8

Chapter 3 Discovering Body Butters..10

Chapter 4 Beauty Within Your Reach 11

Chapter 5 Simple Recipes For A Great Skin 14

Chapter 6 More Tips For A Healthier Skin 17

Conclusion 19

Introduction

I want to thank you and congratulate you for purchasing the book, *"Body Butters For Beginners: Proven Secrets To Making All Natural Body Butters For Rejuvenating And Hydrating Your Skin"*

This book contains proven steps and strategies on how to have radiant and healthy skin with the help of body butters, which you can make all by yourself and at the comfort of your home.

Do you know that having healthy and beautiful skin is as easy as ABC? With simple to follow steps, you can make your own body butters! Whether you are a beginner or an expert chef, you can dish out a body butter recipe for you and your loved ones – not to be eaten of course, but to be applied on the skin. Say goodbye to dry, scaly skin and start giving your skin the star treatment it deserves.

Thanks again for purchasing this book, I hope you enjoy it!

Chapter 1 Deeper Than Skin Deep

Deeper Than Skin Deep

Healthy skin equals a healthy you

Beautiful skin makes all the difference when it comes to total physical beauty. How could it not? The skin is the largest organ of the body and you simply can't avoid seeing it.

When you see famous celebrities in movies and on TV, the first thing you would usually notice about them is their flawless skin. These stars know the importance of taking care of their skin. It is not just superficial for them.

The care for the skin is from inside out. Well, you are a star in your own right and your skin deserves that star treatment as well. You would not regret all the time and finances you spend on taking care of your skin. It would glow and people would know. A healthy skin is something you cannot hide.

How does one achieve an overall great and healthy skin? First, get to know the skin very well. What is it? What is it made of? What does it need?

Your first line of defense

Skin is very important in protecting you and everything inside your body. Imagine, if you do not have skin? It would be gross to see the muscles, bones, and organs all out, wouldn't it? And you would not last long what with all the foreign bodies and infections that might set in to your vital organs.

You could really say that the value of skin is really more than skin deep. It's technically life for everybody. Not only does it protect your body, it also helps your body maintain the right temperature. And without skin how would you be able to feel that tender touch of your loved ones?

Nobody can boast that he or she would survive without the help of the skin. So, maintaining it to be healthy is a must for all. This is, after all, your first line of defense against whatever is the enemy of the body.

What is skin made of? Let's find out.

Parts of skin: three layers

1. Epidermis – the outermost layer. This is what you can see and touch. If you look at the skin on your hand right now, it seems like nothing is going on in there, right? Do not be deceived. Just beneath it is a busy network of different cells and organisms with the sole purpose of making new skin cells. After 2 weeks or a month, these new skin cells would move up to the epidermis. As new cells arise, the old ones die and move on top of the

epidermis where they would be shed off. Around 30k-40k of dead cells are being shed off every minute! Imagine, just by reading this alone, millions of cells have died and have been replaced already in your body. Could the body catch up on replacing these with new cells? You need not worry as the epidermis works 95% all the time to make new skin for you. The other 5% works for melanin. This gives the color of your skin. The darker you are, the more melanin is produced. This keeps you safe from the sun's harmful rays. They make extra melanin to protect you from being sunburned. However, your skin cannot do it alone. It needs you to help protect itself from the destructive effects of the sun. You can do this by applying sunblock or using an umbrella or wearing a hat during a sunny day.

2. Dermis – lies just beneath the epidermis. This is where the blood vessels, nerves, sweat and oil glands are located. There is where you'll find the tough and stretchy collagen and elastin. Nerve endings help you to feel –whether what you have touched was hot or cold. The blood vessels deliver and supply nutrients and oxygen to the skin. Oil or sebaceous glands produce the skin's natural oil called sebum. This body's oil protects and lubricates the skin. Sebum acts as the body's waterproof shield. Have you seen water and oil mix? Sebum makes sure you won't absorb so much water that your skin would be soggy. Sweat glands protect the skin too. They came through pores or the tiny holes in the skin.
3. Subcutaneous fat –the bottom part of the skin, which is mostly made of fat. It helps the body to be warm. It also absorbs shock if you fall down or hit something. This is where the hair follicles are located, too.

Functions of the skin

As you know by now, your skin protects the whole body. It also warms or cools you so that you maintain 37 degrees C or 98.6 degrees F which is the ideal temperature for the body. During a hot day, your body would release heat through the skin to cool you down. So you perspire a lot. When it is cold, your body would preserve heat to keep you warm.

The skin is really deeper than skin deep. It deserves special attention and care. There are many products that can help you moisturize and keep your skin healthy, supple and glowing. Learn more about them as you read on.

Chapter 2 Which Is Which?

Which is which?

Skin care and skin products flood the market. This is a growing industry, which is getting and getting more popular as the years pass. The consumers are sometimes confused which products would benefit them the most.

A lot of people are willing to spend so much just to have beautiful skin. They sometimes commit the error of just buying the most expensive product. Price is not necessarily the basis of how good a skin product is for your skin.

To get the most out of these skin products, you should first know your skin type. There are different skin types. The factors that may affect your skin type include the race, age, weather or season and your overall health status. If you cannot personally determine your skin type, then you can avail the help of the professionals. Your skin is worth it.

Assess your skin type.

There are four skin types– dry, oily, normal and combination.

- Dry skin - this is medically termed as xeroderma. This is due to lack of water on the epidermis. As one ages too, the amount of natural oils and lubricants also diminish which lead to dry skin. The body parts prone to dryness are the arms, elbows, knees, and the lower legs. Aside from ageing, the other causes of dry skin are harsh soaps and other skin products, extreme weather, poor water intake and hot showers.
- Oily skin – the body produces natural oils. For some reasons, some people produce more body oil than what is needed. The following are the possible causes of your oily skin: genes (it runs in your family), overuse of skin products, weather conditions, some drugs, and stress. Oily skin causes acne and skin breakouts. Toners, cleansers, blotting papers and medicated pads are used to manage excessive oily skin.
- Normal skin – some people cannot distinguish if they have normal skin. That is because sometimes, the skin appears oily one time and dry the next. A normal skin has no trace of oil. It feels supple and elastic. And it has the least problem when it comes to skin conditions.
- Combination–this is common and in the face, it could be that some parts are oily (usually the nose and forehead) and some are dry, like the cheeks.

Various skin products

Now that you are aware of the type of skin that you have, you go to the next step. Determine which product your skin needs. You are already aware that your skin's primary need is hydration. There are different hydration elements. The two most common are humectant and lubricant.

- Humectant –these retain or preserve the moisture
- Lubricant – "trap" moisture or prevent it from escaping, serving as a barrier to the skin

While both lotions and moisturizers possess these elements, not all products containing these would automatically make your skin healthy. Lotions are less viscous, meaning they are more fluid-like and thinner. They have lighter consistency. This is why they are usually in a container where you can pump it. Lotions can retain moisture that is already within the skin but not as much. They have less oil content so they do not lubricate well. For normal skin, these products would suffice.

However, for drier skin, you would need added protection and moisture-retaining products. For those individuals who have extra-dry skin, even the strongest lotion would not be enough to combat the dryness. You might want to consider trying body butters.

Know more about this skin wonder product as you read on.

Chapter 3 Discovering Body Butters

Discovering Body Butters

What are body butters?

You may not be aware of body butters. These are actually moisturizers that contain lubricating ingredients. They are technically like lotions, only better. These ingredients serve as a protective barrier or a shield so that moisture would stay within the skin and outside environmental elements that may be harmful to the skin would not be able to come in.

Body butters are more emollient, have high viscosity and more effective for those with dry skin. Some examples of these lubricating ingredients are shea butter, coconut oil, olive and jojoba oils. Consumers also describe body butters as ensuring a "more luxurious" feel on their skin.

Body butters are extra moisturizing because they contain less water and have more essential oils or butters needed by the body to maintain moisture. Viscosity and consistency are greater so these butters are placed in jars where they would be scooped, because it would be difficult to pump them out.

Another wonder of body butter is it is ideal for those with sensitive skin. Allergies or rashes seldom occur because the ingredients of body butters are all-natural. Usually, a body butter is made up of an oil base and a few more ingredients. You would appreciate the fact that they are free from various chemicals and preservatives that could harm your skin.

Do you want to know another wonder of body butters? You could actually make your own right at the comfort of your home. They are easy to make and the ingredients are not hard to find, too.

Are you ready for a healthier skin? Find out more about making your own body butters.

Chapter 4 Beauty Within Your Reach

Beauty Within Your Reach

It is time to end the confusion on which products suit you. It is time to make your own body butters.

One great thing about body butters is the availability of the ingredients. You could avail of these even from your local stores. You would notice though that the ingredients are mostly derived from nuts and seeds. So if you have allergies to these, it is wise to consult your primary health care provider first just to be sure if topical applications would be hazardous to you.

Here are some of the basic ingredients of body butter.

1. Cocoa butter – Cocoa butter is made from cocoa beans. Cocoa beans come from the fleshy cocoa fruits. After cleaning and roasting, the beans are placed in a machine where the cocoa butter would be produced. Of course, in your local store, you could just buy it as a cocoa butter already. This is actually a vegetable fat that is edible. It is used mostly for making chocolates and beauty products. What makes this as a good ingredient to help your skin? The cocoa itself contains large amounts of antioxidants called flavonoids. It is also rich in potassium, calcium and iron. These allow veins to be more relaxed. This promotes good circulation and at the same time, help fight against free radicals that are harmful to the body. Not to mention, this smells good too.

2. Shea butter – Another common ingredient of body butter is shea butter. This comes from the nut of the African shea tree or karite tree. This is also known as karite butter. Like the cocoa butter, this extracted fat is also edible and can be used in making chocolates. This ingredient has been known to be very effective in the fight against stretch marks. It has been internationally recognized to treat various skin disorders as well. This is because it has been found to contain anti-inflammatory properties. It is also an anti-ageing agent. The vitamins found in shea butter help in preventing the occurrence of wrinkles and other facial lines. Plus it can be a form of sunblock and even as a relief for nasal congestion and sinusitis.

3. Coconut oil – Much has been written about the wonders of this ingredient. In some tropical areas, the coconut tree is considered as the tree of life. It has been used for thousands of years not only as skin beautifier but as supplements to help conquer Alzheimer disease, Diabetes Mellitus, Thyroid problems, weight concerns and even hair problems like lice and dandruff.

Coconut is known to be the number one source of lauric acids. These acids have been known to fight off pathogens or harmful organisms in the body.

4. Mango butter – Another great ingredient is mango butter which is an oil extracted from the kernel of a mango. It has anti-inflammatory, anti-oxidant and anti-ageing properties, making it a favorite among cosmetics suppliers. It contains oleic and stearic acids in very large amounts. These make mango butter highly emollient and thus ideal in sealing moisture within the body. It highly nourishes the skin, too. Plus it has a very sweet and refreshing smell. Mango butter can also provide protection from the sun. It also non-greasy and very soothing to touch.

5. Cinnamon – The common kitchen ingredient cinnamon has some uncommon qualities. Do you know that it is a proven antimicrobial, anti-fungal and antibacterial agent? What's more, it has an astringent property, which helps make the skin firmer and clearer as it removes blemishes. Cinnamon is gaining popularity because it is also very rich in magnesium, iron and calcium. These are minerals that help keep skin healthy. Cinnamon is great for body butters as it also helps local blood circulation. A good circulation allows for delivery of nutrients and oxygen to the different parts of the body. This has been used in the fight against acne and has shown to remove impurities and to aid as an anti inflammatory substance as well.

6. Honey – Raw honey is a humectant. It helps retain water so that the skin is kept moisturized. Honey as a cosmetic agent has been used for thousands of years already. It was discovered to contain skin restorative properties. Just a little amount can go a long way in making the skin youthful looking. Honey also contains germ-fighting bacteria, which help in fighting off the enemies of the skin.

7. Other ingredients – do not be surprise that other nuts and seeds can be included as ingredients too in any body butter that you could make. As long as there is the base oil or lubricant, you could add other ingredients that could enhance the feel, the smell and the color of the body butter. These are peppermint, rosemary, lavender, magnesium, black raspberry, coffee, cinnamon, vanilla, lemon, avocado and the list goes on.

You can enjoy tremendous peace of mind since you are 100% sure that what you are using won't harm your skin or make it look unsightly. With these ingredients, you could start making your own body butter now. Plus it can also be a great gift idea for your family and friends.

Having healthy skin need not be difficult nor expensive. Start having great skin that you could show off! Start making your own body butters.

Chapter 5 Simple Recipes For A Great Skin

Simple Recipes For Great Skin

Do you know that you can make as many as one hundred or more different body butters for your skin? That's right, and all these at the comfort of your own home with no special machinery needed. You do not even have to be a chef to do these. You could be a beginner and a master at making body butters at the same time.

Here are simple tips before you start.

1. Remember to check if you have any allergic reaction or even sensitivity to any of the ingredients that you are going to use. If unsure, it is better to try it out on a small portion of your arm first. If there are no untoward reactions, such as itchiness, redness, warm feeling or any sign of irritation, then you can try it on other parts until you have proven that it is safe for you.
2. Melting the oils is one basic action in making your own body butter. Try to melt it slowly by using low to medium level of heat. Do not place the oil at a high level of heat at any time.
3. You would also be asked to chill or set the oil. This is allowing the oils to cool and then form into a semi-solid state. If you would set it in a room temperature, it could take hours. In the refrigerator, estimated time for the oils to set is 15-20 minutes. Chilling properly is important because you would not want it to be frozen. It could kill some of the vitamins and minerals on the oils, rendering it useless. And you would also have difficulty in getting the right viscosity of the body butter.
4. Finally, you would be asked to whip it until it reaches the butter-like consistency.

The body butters should be placed on clean glass jars.

The finished product should be maintained at a cool temperature to keep if from melting. However, if it melts, simply stir or whip it again until it returns to its previous consistency.

The homemade product's lifespan depends on many factors, but to be on the safe side, try to use it for three months at the most. There are reports of 6 months up to a year of useful life for these products.

Cooking Time

It is time to start making those body butters. Here are 10 simple recipes that you could use.

1. Triple delight body butter – Simply melt 1 cup shea butter and ½ cup coconut oil in the top of a double boiler. Once melted, allow the mixture to

cool for 30 minutes. Stir in the half cup of almond oil. Place in the freezer or chiller (this is very important – chilling should just be right. It is about 20 minutes). Whip into a butter-like consistency when the oil starts to partially become solid. Place in a clean jar and then use for hydrating and rejuvenating your skin. Keep in a cool place. Simple right?

2. Vanilla Secret Body Butter – Do you know that vanilla can serve as aphrodisiac? Feel sexier as you use this body butter. Melt a cup of cocoa butter and half cup of coconut oil. Remove from heat and allow to cool for thirty minutes. While waiting to cool, grind in a coffee grinder (or you could also use a food processor) a single vanilla bean. Place in a container. Stir in half cup of sweet almond oil into the vanilla bits plus the cooled oil mixture. Place in a freezer to chill. Wait until the oils start to be partially solid. Then using an electric mixer or a food processor, whip until it becomes like butter. There you have a vanilla body butter, which you could use to attract your partner too.

3. Mango & Shea Body Butter - Combine the following ingredients in a double boiler – ½ cup shea butter, ½ cup mango butter, ½ cup coconut oil and ½ cup olive or jojoba. Constantly stir as you melt all the oils. Remove from heat and allow to cool for 30 minutes. Place in the freezer until it starts to harden but it is still soft. Whip until fluffy and there you have it! Your own body butter for a more beautiful skin!

4. Rose Scented Coconut body butter – As you melt, cool and place the cup of coconut oil in the freezer, just add a few drops of rose scented oil to perfect the moisturizer. When in a semi solid stage, whip until it becomes butter-like in consistency. You would not only have a soft skin but you would simply adore that perfume like smell.

5. No-cook body butter – place all the ingredients in a food processor or blender. These are ¾ cup melted coconut oil, ½ tablespoons vanilla powder, ¼ cup cacao powder and 1/3 cup clear agave. Blend and then place them in clean glass or jars and then place in the refrigerator to set in.

6. Fruity body butter – combine half cup each of cocoa and shea butters. Melt and allow to cool. Add around 10-20 drops (depends on how fruity you like it to smell) of Black Raspberry Fragrance Oil. Place in the refrigerator to set it. Once it is almost solid, whip it until it becomes like butter in consistency. You will then have a body butter that smells so cool.

7. Lemony Body Butters – Place 6 tablespoons coconut oil and ¼ cup cacao butter in a saucepan and melt it. Remove from heat and add 1 teaspoon lemon essential oil. Cool until the mixture solidifies. Whip and it is ready to use. You would love its refreshing lemon smell.

8. Pretty in Pink Body butter – this is a great idea for a gift. It looks charming with its pink color too. Melt 6 ounces coconut oil and 2 ounces cocoa butter in a low heat double boiler. After melting, remove from heat and let it cool. You could make this faster by placing it in the refrigerator. Once it is partially solid, you can whip this manually or use an electric mixer. The oils would turn creamy. Place this creamy oil in the refrigerator again for five minutes and then whip again. At this point, you could add essential oil like rosemary or peppermint until you get stiff peaks. As it is, it is already

attractive and healthy for your skin. However, you could make it daintier by adding red colorant to the finished product, giving it a pinkish shade.

9. Glowing Skin Body Butter – the secret to this recipe is the use of extra virgin, raw and organic coconut oil. The feel afterwards is extra smooth and soft skin. Like the other recipes, just add this special 2 cups of coconut oil and 7 ounces of shea butter and allow to melt in a saucepan. Cool and at this time, you could add a drop of tea tree oil. Tea tree oil is known for its antimicrobial and antibacterial properties. You could also add any essential oils that you like. Peppermint, jasmine or rosemary smells great on this combination. This is optional though. Cool, set in and then whip. You now have a body butter that is sure to make your skin healthier and softer.

10. Cinnamon Power Packed Body Butter – Melt 50 grams cocoa butter and 50 grams shea butter until it becomes a liquid. Add 100 grams coconut oil, stir in gently for a minute and then remove the oils from heat. Let it cool for 30 minutes. Add 30 drops of cinnamon oil as soon as it cools. Then whip until it becomes fluffy and butter-like. Before pouring it to containers, add some bits of cinnamon stick on it. Preferable containers are airtight.

That was easy, right? Even a first timer would get it right. You could do some mixing and matching of ingredients and you could even invent your own body butter. Make your own until you find the one that suits you perfectly. You would know if it is the perfect one for you when your skin feels so soft and smooth. You would also notice that your skin looks hydrated. This is because the moisture is locked in.

It is also recommended that you try and change the skin products every six months. This is to have a variety of available minerals and vitamins for your skin. Changing your body butters would also allow you to enjoy different smells and effects on your skin.

Chapter 6 More Tips For A Healthier Skin

More Tips For A Healthier Skin

Healthy Radiant Skin

Body butters and other moisturizers are big help when it comes to rejuvenated and hydrated skin. However, there are other things you could do to ensure a healthier skin.

Basic care for the skin

Caring for the skin cannot be overemphasized. Here are some simple things you can do to care for your skin.

1. Clean according to skin type. Different skin types require different kind of cleaning. For dry skin, use a mild cleansing product and clean only once, preferably at night. For oily skin, you could wash and clean it twice in a day. For the combination type, combine also the style of cleansing. For normal skin, regular washing would do. Follow the instructions on the labels of the products carefully.
2. Remove all make up. As much as possible, allow your skin to rest by not wearing any make up. If you do need to wear makeup, make sure that you totally remove it at the end of the day by washing thoroughly. Pat dry.
3. Protection from the sun. Your skin's number one enemy is the sun, although the sun is a friend from 7-8am. Afterwards, try to avoid its harmful rays as much as possible. You could apply sunscreen, use umbrella or wear clothes with sleeves.
4. Exfoliate. This simply means to remove the dead skin (you have millions of them remember?). You could do this on skin without breaks. There are products available in your local grocery store for exfoliation. Follow the instructions very well.
5. Water. When you think of skin, you want it to be hydrated at all times. By simply drinking 8-10 glasses a day, you are already helping your skin to be hydrated and radiant.
6. Do not scratch, pick on pimples, remove scabs or do anything that would break the skin. Keep it intact at all cost. You should also try to trim your nails so that they would not cause damage to your skin.
7. Supplements to help. Aside from eating healthy foods like fruits and vegetables, vitamins a, b, c and e can also help skin become healthier, softer and more beautiful.
8. Healthy lifestyle. Drinking alcoholic beverages, sleeping late, smoking, and eating junk foods are just some of the way that would harm your skin. Try having healthy habits and get enough rest and sleep.
9. Lotions and other products. To keep your skin from drying or just to moisturize it, there are various products that you can choose from and use.

Find which one suits you best. Extreme weathers would require that you use these products more often to protect your skin.

A healthy skin is a goal that everybody must have. Skin care is easy and the rewards are awesome. Hydrated and rejuvenated skin looks great and at the same time, it is a great protector of the body. Enjoy a smooth and flawless skin now!

Conclusion

Thank you again for purchasing this book!

I hope this book was able to help you to start having great skin with very little efforts and cost by making your all-natural, easy to make body butters.

The next step is to enjoy that flawless and smooth skin. Share the secret to others too, by sharing this book to them.

Finally, if you enjoyed this book, please take the time to share your thoughts and post a review on Amazon. We do our best to reach out to readers and provide the best value we can. Your positive review will help us achieve that. It'd be greatly appreciated!

Thank you and good luck!

Book 2

Soap Making For Beginners
BY LINDSEY P

A Guide to Making Natural Homemade Soaps from Scratch, Includes Recipes and Step by Step Processes for Making Soaps

Table Of Contents

Introduction 23

Chapter 1 - Hello, Soap Making Starter! 24

Chapter 2 - Get to Know the Basic Tools and Ingredients of Soap Making 26

Chapter 3 - Soap Making Made Easy by SoapCalc 32

Chapter 4 - Cold Process Soap 34

Chapter 5 - Hot Process Soap 37

Conclusion 40

Check Out My Other Books 41

Introduction

I want to thank you and congratulate you for purchasing the book, "Soap Making For Beginners: A Guide To Making Natural Homemade Soaps From Scratch, Includes Recipes and Step By Step Processes for Making Soaps."

This book contains proven steps and strategies on how to create natural homemade soaps using easy to obtain ingredients.

This book is perfect for those who want to make their own soap but do not know where to begin. Soap making is a fun and rewarding hobby that you can also turn into a business once you have successfully made your first batch of soap. In this book, you will get to know the different ingredients, tools and processes on how to create soap.

Thanks again for purchasing this book, I hope you enjoy it!

Chapter 1 - Hello, Soap Making Starter!

Making your own batch of natural soap at home has many advantages. First of all, you get to enjoy hypoallergenic soap that can even clear up facial acne and skin blemishes. The perfectly processed soap acts as a gentle cleanser and moisturizer that is fun to make and pleasurable to use.

How Soap is Formed

Soap forms when lye and water chemically react together with oil, turning the oil into a salt. This is known as "saponification." Lye should be slowly added (never poured!) into the water. Once you add the lye and water to the oil, the mixture will start to thicken, and the primary stage of this thickening is referred to as "light trace". The "gel stage" takes place once the soap becomes so heated up that it starts to look like applesauce. This is full saponification and it means that the soap is almost completely formed. It will keep on thickening until it becomes a solid bar.

There are two types of process in forming soap, and these are cold process and hot process (you will know more about them in chapter 3). It takes around 24 to 48 hours for the saponification to occur in cold process soap, while in hot process the soap will have already saponified after it is done cooking.

Solid soaps are formed with "alkalis", while liquid soap are formed with potassium hydroxide. These ingredients are dangerous if not handled properly.

You should only use pure lye that is specifically for making soap. You can buy this online or you can use Red Devil lye. If you do not want to use lye you can opt for the melt and pour soap, which is a finished soap product with directions on how to process it.

Soaps' shelf life depends a lot on their ingredients, particularly the iodine value. Some soaps can last for years, while others do not last for over twelve months. If the iodine in the soap is too high it will create what are called "dreaded orange spots" or DOS, which is a sign that the soap is stale. You will learn about how to calculate the ingredients in your soap carefully using a soap calculator (soapcalc.net), including the iodine value.

To keep soap fresh, it is recommended that you keep it in a closed plastic container such as a plastic shoe box. Soap can absorb scents quickly, and you do not want it to absorb other scents apart from the one that you used with it.

Soap Making Safety Equipment

Soap making should be done in a room wherein you will not be disturbed by your kids, visitors or pets. You will also need a few basic and inexpensive safety equipment to keep yourself safe. These are:

Gloves. You will need latex gloves like the ones being used by doctors. These are inexpensive and can be found in any drugstore.

Safety Goggles or Face Shield. Wear a pair of safety goggles that are resistant to heat and will wrap around your eyes completely. If you wear glasses, then you can opt for the full face shield instead. Both are relatively inexpensive and can be found in any hardware store.

Long-sleeved Shirt and Apron. You will need to protect your skin and clothes from lye and potassium hydroxide for these can irritate the skin and burn a hole upon contact on your clothing.

Shoes. Always wear shoes - never wear slippers, sandals nor go barefoot - while making soap. Any spills or splatters will burn your skin. Wear a pair of closed shoes which you won't mind getting splattered on.

Vinegar. This is more of a first aid item that you need to have at hand because it neutralizes lye. If any lye splatters onto your skin, immediately wash it off with water and pour vinegar onto it to remove all traces.

In the next chapter, you will get to know the different basic ingredients and tools that you will need in making natural soap.

Chapter 2 - Get to Know the Basic Tools and Ingredients of Soap Making

In preparing for soap making, make sure that the venue is off limits to other people, especially kids and pets. After all, you do not want to risk any injuries. Now let's jump right into the list of tools and ingredients that you will need for your soap making project.

Basic Tools

The tools that you will need in making soap are inexpensive and easy to obtain. These are:

Handheld immersion blender. This type of blender is sticklike with a spinning blade on one end. This is used mostly for drinks or whipping cream but in this case you will be using it for making soap. It helps minimize the energy spent on stirring but you can skip this if your arm is used to stirring for extended periods of time.

Stainless steel stockpot with lid. If you already have one in your kitchen you can use that. It needs to be very clean and still be safe enough to cook food in. Ideally, it should hold from three to twelve quarts to create a nice batch of soap. Never use aluminum or enamel-ware pots because the lye will eat through these types of material.

Bowls. Use only plastic or stainless steel bowls while measuring your soap ingredients. You can also use a plastic pitcher (never glass!) that has a lid to mix lye.

Whisk or spoon and Spatula. Only use a whisk or spoon made of stainless steel or the kind made for using with nonstick pans. Do not use wooden.

Scale. You will need a quality electronic kitchen scale with a platform that can any of the bowls and pitchers that you will be using. It should measure to 1/10 an ounce and should also measure in grams.

Stainless steel thermometer. You will need this to check the oils', lye and water temperature to find out the right time to mix the oils with the lye and water. If you do not have a thermometer, you can touch the outside of the pitcher or pot using your fingers. You will know when the lye and water can be added to the oil once the heat is bearable to the touch.

Soap Molds. Any container except metal can be used as a soap mold. Some suggestions would be plastic tray molds with cute designs on top. A 5x6 inch container can hold 1.5 pounds or 24 ounces of soap. There are plenty of wooden, acrylic and plastic soap molds that you can shop for online with a wide variety of designs to choose from.

Basic Ingredients

You do not need a lot of ingredients to create a simple bar of natural soap. Here is an overview:

Oils and butters. These work as the bases of the soap. The different oils and butters have varied properties with specific uses. Base oils are palm oil, lard and tallow. Cleansing oils are palm kernel, babassu, and coconut oil. For lather and moisturizing, use Castor oil.

Lye. You cannot make soap without lye. Sodium hydroxide is used for creating solid (bar) soap while potassium hydroxide is used for creating liquid soap. Lye produces a toxic vapor when it is added and stirred into the water. Make sure that your room is well-ventilated and you are wearing a protective mask.

Borax. This ingredient is needed to neutralize the leftover lye in liquid soap, lower the pH, and improve its cleaning power. It is also a deodorizer and disinfectant.

Additives

Naturally you would want your soap to be a lot more fun than just the basic bar. There are plenty of additives that you can incorporate into your soap mixture such as fragrance, milk, honey, herbs and so on.

If you wish to use fragrance oils, use only those that are guaranteed safe for the skin. Essential oils can be used but must be at a minimum (about a maximum of 2.5 percent) because too much of this can irritate the skin.

You can also use liquid colorants to make you soap look more attractive. Just make sure to use the kind that is safe on the skin such as micas or oxides.

Choosing Oils and Butters

As a soap making starter, shea butter is an excellent type of butter that is great for soap making. It has moisturizing properties that can also increase lather. Three basic oils for soap making are coconut oil, castor oil, and palm oil.

There are plenty of other oils and butters that you can use for soap making as well. Here is a list:

- Almond Oil
- Apricot Kernel Oil
- Avocado Oil

- Babassu Oil
- Canola Oil
- Castor Oil
- Cocoa Butter
- Corn Oil
- Emu Oil
- Flaxseed Oil
- Grapeseed Oil
- Hemp Seed Oil
- Illipe Butter
- Jojoba Oil
- Karanja Oil
- Kokum Butter
- Lanolin
- Lard
- Mango Butter
- Mowrah Butter
- Neem Seed Oil
- Olive Oil
- Olive Oil Pomace
- Ostrich Oil
- Palm Oil
- Palm Kernel Oil
- Peanut Oil
- Rice Bran Oil
- Safflower Oil (High Oleic)
- Sal Butter

- Shea Butter

- Soybean Oil

- Sunflower Oil (High Oleic)

- Beef Tallow

Do some more research on each oil and butter on your own and you will find an encyclopedia of benefits along with specific properties. Most of these oils and butters can be bought in your local grocery store.

Fragrances

To add scent to your soap, you can make use of fragrances or essential oils. Fragrance oils are synthetic blends made up of chemicals that copy the scents of essential oils. Below is a list of the most commonly used fragrances:

- Spellbound Woods

- Black Tea and Berries

- Cool Mountain Lake

- Lavender Rose

- Cucumber Mint

- Hardwood Musk

- Fresh Pomegranate

Keep in mind that there are close to 8,000 fragrances available on the market. Have fun trying them all! Just make sure to use skin-safe and avoid the ones containing the chemical called "phthalates" because these are harmful to your skin. Opt for higher quality oils because the scent will last much longer even if they are more expensive. You can use about .5 to .7 ounce of strong fragrance oil per pound of oil compared to using 1 ounce per pound of oil if you use cheaper fragrance oil.

Essential Oils

Essential oils do not just smell good but they also have medicinal properties. They are distilled from bark, flower, roots, stems or leaves of plants and can be too potent, so use sparingly. Here is a list of essential oils commonly used in soap making:

- Balsam Peru

- Sweet Basil
- Bay laurel
- Bay rum
- Benzoin
- Bergamot
- Cajeput
- Carrot Seed
- Cedarwood, atlas
- Cinnamon bark
- Clary sage
- Combava petitgrain
- Coriander
- Cypress
- Elemi
- Eucalyptus
- Eucalyptus, lemon
- Fir Needle
- Frankincense
- Geranium
- Grapefruit, pink
- Jasmine
- Juniper berry
- Lavender
- Lemongrass
- Manuka
- Myrrh
- Myrtle

- Neroli
- Niaouli
- Oak moss absolute
- Bitter Orange
- Oregano
- Patchouli
- Peppermint
- Rosalina
- Rosemary
- Rosewood
- Sage
- Spearmint
- Spikenard
- Spruce
- Stryax resin
- Tangerine
- Tea tree
- Thyme
- Verbena
- Vetiver, El Salvador
- Violet leaf
- Yarrow
- Ylang ylang

Do extensive research on each essential oil and you will find a wide range of medicinal benefits. Many of these essential oils have natural antibacterial properties. Just make sure not to use peppermint essential oil on diabetics and be careful in selecting the right essential oils for infants younger than 3 months as well as pregnant women. You can blend your essential oils and be as creative as you like.

Chapter 3 - Soap Making Made Easy by SoapCalc

Soon you will get to know the basic steps on how to process soap. There are mainly two basic processes, the Hot Process and Cold Process. But before moving on to these two, let's first discuss a very useful online tool that you can use in formulating the perfect soap recipes.

Using SoapCalc

It is very easy to formulate the kind of soap that you would like to create. All you will need is a computer or Smart Phone and internet connection. Visit www.soapcalc.net and all of the instructions will be given to you there.

In SoapCalc, all you have to do is to type in the ingredients and to pick the qualities that you would like for your soap. After clicking a button, SoapCalc will give you the recipe and recommendations on the right amount of water and lye that you will need to get the recipe that you want..

If it all seems too confusing at first, you can start practicing with this basic soap recipe:

Basic soap is made up of 70 percent Palm oil, 20 percent coconut oil, and 10 percent castor oil.

Step 1: in Box 2 in soapcalc.net, click on the "Ounces" button (box 6 will change to "oz.") and type in "11".

Step 2: in Box 3, convert the "Water as % of Oils" from default (which is 38 percent) to 30.

Step 3: in Box 4, convert the "Super Fat %" to "10", and for fragrance, type ".5".

Step 4: In the list of oils, double click on "Palm". Click the circle over the "%" and the column will turn green. Type in "70" beside Palm.

Step 5: Double click on "Coconut (76 deg, solid) and then, in the green field beneath %, type in "20".

Step 6: Double click "Castor Oil" and add "10" in the green field.

Step 7: In Box 8, click the "Calculate Recipe".

If you do not get 100 percent, you will see a pop-up box that will show how much you need to add or subtract in order to get 100 percent.

You will see a "View or Print Recipe" button. Once you click it, you will see your soap recipe in a new window.

Find the time to explore soapcalc.net in order to familiarize yourself with its features. Once you start working on your own first batch of soap, you are most likely to be successful while using this tool.

Chapter 4 - Cold Process Soap

Cold Process or CP soap is when the saponification happens while the mixture is in the mold. It takes longer for the soap to cure this way compared to the Hot Process. "Curing" is the state wherein the water evaporates and the soap would harden.

The first part of the process is to mix fixed oils (such as Palm, Coconut or Olive) with alkali (lye or Sodium hydroxide). After that you bring the batch to trace. "Trace" is the state wherein the soap batch thickens. There are 3 trace stages, and these are light, medium, and thick. The moment trace begins, you will notice a ripple when you check the back of your spoon or immersion blender while you move it through the mixture. Light trace will have the consistency of thin sauce. Medium trace has the consistency of gravy. Thick trace will be similar to a pudding.

Once it is in the Medium stage of trace, you pour the mixture into the mold and use wax paper to cover it. Finally, you set it aside to solidify.

Cold process soap will have a texture that is creamier compared to hot process soap. Choosing this process will also enable you to be in complete control over the ingredients. Most often, the soaps will have a longer shelf life as well. One disadvantage is that it takes from four to six weeks of curing time. Because of this, some essential oils and fragrance oils do not outlast the cold process and would undergo chemical decomposition.

Cold Process Oven Process. A modified CP method called the Cold Process Oven Process or CPOP method is a great way to reap the benefits of CP soap without the extended waiting time. Certain batches can cure for only two or three days. The only change that you need to do in the cold process soap instructions is to not just set the soap-filled mold aside, but to put it in the oven.

Right before mixing the ingredients, preheat your oven to 170 degrees Fahrenheit (76.67 degrees Celsius). After you have mixed the lye and oils and poured it into the mold, cover it with wax paper. Next, you turn off the oven but keep the oven light on. After that, you place the mold into the oven and let it sit there for a few hours to cool. Remove the soap once it is hard enough and cut into bars. After that, let it sit for a few more days.

It is ideal to let the soap sit for 48 hours before the soap is taken out of the mold and set on a drying rack. The soap should be left to dry for another 24 to 48 hours before it is cut into bars. Soap is typically cut at 3.25 inches in length and 2.25 inches in width.

How to Make Cold Process Soap

To create CP soap, prepare all of the safety tools and soap making equipment along with some freezer paper, wax paper, paper towels, and a stove. The ingredients you will need are the following: oil, skin-safe fragrance or essential oil, soap-safe colorant, sodium hydroxide lye, and distilled water. For each pound of soap you will need 11 ounces of oils. The rest will be made up of lye and water.

The following recipe will yield 3 pounds of soap. Type in the following information in SoapCalc:

Weight of Oils - 33 ounces

Water as % of Oils - 38

Super Fat % - 5

Fragrance Oz per Lb - 1

Distilled water - 12.5 oz (355.5 g)

Lye - sodium hydroxide - 4.6 oz (131.0 g)

Castor oil - 6.6 oz (186.1 g) (20%)

Coconut oil (76 degrees) - 6.6 oz (187.1 g) 20%

Palm oil - 19.8 oz (561.3 g) (60%)

The soap qualities will then be:

Hardness - 46

Cleansing - 14

Conditioning - 51

Bubbly - 32

Creamy - 50

Iodine - 51

INS - 156

The following are steps on how to create Basic Cold Process Soap. Remember to wear your safety glasses and latex gloves whenever you are about to handle lye and lye mixtures.

Step 1: With the shiny side up, use freezer paper to line the mold unless your mold is made of plastic.

Step 2: Set your measuring scale to ounces or grams, and place a clean empty plastic pitcher on top. After that, press the tare button to remove the pitcher's weight so that the scale will show zero. Pour water into the pitcher until you get 12.5 oz (255.5 g). Remove the pitcher and set aside.

Step 3: Put a bowl on the scale and do the same process to zero out the bowl's weight. Use a scoop or spoon to add the lye into the bowl until you get 4.6 oz (131.0 g). Remove the bowl and set aside.

Step 4: In a well-ventilated area (such as near a window or extracting fan), place the pitcher of water on a counter or sink and then very slowly add the lye to the water while stirring. Keep stirring until the lye is completely dissolved. This will make the water hot.

Step 5: Place this lye/water mixture in a secure area to cool for about 60 minutes.

Step 6: Melt and stir your palm oil on top of a stove in a stainless steel pot. It is essential to melt the oil before weighing it.

Step 7: Weight 19.8 oz (561.3 g) of the melted palm oil on your scale in a separate clean stainless steel pot. Repeat the process with castor oil for 6.6 oz (187.1 g) and coconut oil for 6.6 oz (187.1 g).

Step 8: Using a steel thermometer, check if the lye and oils have cooled to lower than 90 degrees Fahrenheit (32.22 degrees Celsius). If they are, then you can very slowly pour the lye/water mixture into the oils.

Step 9: Carefully blend the lye/water and oils together with your stainless steel spoon or blender. After they are blended well together you can add your fragrance.

Step 10: Keep stirring until you begin seeing trace. Once it gets to a Medium trace you can pour the mixture into your prepared mold. Be careful not to stir it too much such that it will reach the Thick trace; this will be very difficult to transfer into the mold.

Step 11: Cover your soap-filled mold with waxed paper or the lid of your plastic try. Let it sit for 48 hours. This will give it enough time to go through the gel stage.

Step 12: After 48 hours, you can take the soap out of the mold and transfer it to a flat surface lined with waxed paper. Let the soap air for a couple more hours before you cut them up into bars. Make sure to wear latex gloves as the lye is still active and will irritate your skin.

Step 13: Let the soap cure and completely harden before use. To test whether the lye has completely neutralized, you can do the "zap test". Very quickly tap the soap to the tip of your tongue. If the soap is just bitter (with that soapy taste), then it is good to go. If there is a slight tingle or "zap" on your tongue, it means the lye is still active and will need more time to cure.

Chapter 5 - Hot Process Soap

Hot process is a method that will produce soap instantly or with minimal cure time compared to cold compress sop. It requires you to cook the soap mixture on the stove until it fully saponifies. Set it aside and let it cool, and right after that you can start using it.

The latest instructions on how to do hot process soap is to begin with the steps in creating cold process oven process soap. The oven is also preheated to 170 degrees Fahrenheit but this time, you do not turn off the oven as you put the soap-filled mold inside of it. Let it cook at the same temperature for 4 hours. After that, you turn off the heat but do not remove the mold. Let the oven cool completely before you do so. The moment you take it out of the oven, you can cut and then use the bars immediately.

The disadvantage to using hot process is that it can be difficult to remove the soap from the mold. To make this task easier for you, what you do is to line the mold with freezer paper (shiny side up) before you pour the soap mixture into the mold. At the end of the process, the soap will not be difficult to remove from the mold.

How to Make Hot Process Soap

Prepare all of the safety and soap making equipment, along with a 2 cup measuring cup, a ceramic bowl and a stove with an oven. The following will be a basic soap recipe that will yield 17.11 oz (485.1 g) of soap.

First start with SoapCalc and type in the following details:

Weight of Oils - 11 oz

Water as % of Oils - 38

Super Fat - 8

Fragrance Oz per Lb - .7

Distilled water - 4.18 oz (118.503 g)

Lye - sodium hydroxide - 1.454 oz (41.232 g)

Beef tallow - 7.92 oz (224.532 g) (72%)

Coconut oil - 1.10 oz (31.185 g) (10%)

Castor oil - 1.10 oz (31.185 g) (10%)

Fragrance oil - .481 oz (13.640 g)

The soap qualities will then be:

Hardness - 50

Cleansing - 11

Conditioning - 48

Bubbly - 20

Creamy - 47

Iodine - 50

INS - 146

The following are steps on how to create Basic Hot Process Soap. Remember to wear your safety glasses and latex gloves whenever you are about to handle lye and lye mixtures.

Step 1: With the shiny side up, use freezer paper to line the mold unless your mold is made of plastic.

Step 2: Set your measuring scale to ounces or grams, and place the ceramic bowl on top. After that, press the tare button to remove the pitcher's weight so that the scale will show zero. Pour fragrance oil into the ceramic bowl until you get .481 oz (13.640 g). Remove the bowl and set aside.

Step 3: Put a larger bowl on the scale and push the tare button again. Weight every oil separately and add them to the stainless steel pot.

Step 4: Place the pot full of oils over medium to low heat. Allow the oils to melt completely.

Step 5: As the oils continue to be heated, put a plastic bowl on top of the scale and zero out its weight by pressing the tare button. Weight the sodium hydroxide or lye in the bowl and then set it aside.

Step 6: Put a pitcher on the scale and zero out its weight. Pour distilled water into it and weigh it, then set aside.

Step 7: After the oils are thoroughly melted, mix the lye very carefully with the water. Ensure that you are wearing your safety glasses and latex gloves. Remember to do this in a well-ventilated area as well. The lye should be sprinkled slowly into the water while stirring. Keep your face as far from the pitcher as possible because the vapors are toxic.

Step 8: Keep the pot heated over medium to low heat as you pour the lye/water mixture in with the oils. Use your immersion blender to mix all of the ingredients thoroughly

Step 9: Keep on stirring while the pot is on the stove. You will notice the soap starting to trace. Keep it heated. You will eventually notice the oils separating and floating to the top. Continue to cook until the soap mixture starts to smooth out.

Step 10: As soon as the soap mixture will turn into a mashed potato consistency, add your fragrance and stir it thoroughly. If you wish to add soap-safe colorant into your soap mixture, scoop out roughly 1 cup of the soap and add it to the bowl holding your colorant. Mix them well until the entire soap mixture is evenly tinted. Pour this back into the pot and stir until you get the effect that you want.

Step 11: Transfer the soap into your mold. Make it as smooth as you can on top. Tap the soap-filled mold onto a flat surface to force any air bubbles out. Set the mold aside to let the soap cool in room temperature.

Step 12: Once the soap is thoroughly cool, cut it into bars for use. Use a soap cutter or a long knife to do this. To cut cleanly, position yourself directly over the soap and cut straight down in one swift push.

Once you have finished making your first batch of soap, you will find that the process is not that hard. It does take a bit of patience and utmost accuracy, but the results will definitely be worth it. After you have tried any one of the recipes in this book, you can try out plenty more soap recipes that you can find on the internet or in soap making books.

Have fun with your new soap making hobby!

Conclusion

Thank you again for purchasing this book!

I hope this book was able to help you to understand what you need in order to start making natural homemade soap at home.

The next step is to start processing your first batch of soap.

Finally, if you enjoyed this book, please take the time to share your thoughts and post a review on Amazon. We do our best to reach out to readers and provide the best value we can. Your positive review will help us achieve that. It'd be greatly appreciated!

Thank you and good luck!

Check Out My Other Books

Below you'll find some of my other popular books that are popular on Amazon and Kindle as well. Simply click on the links below to check them out. Alternatively, you can visit my author page on Amazon to see other work done by me.

Coconut Oil for Easy Weight Loss

http://amzn.to/1i5f45p

Carrier Oils For Beginners

http://amzn.to/1sbqUQP

Natural Homemade Cleaning Recipes For Beginners

http://amzn.to/1izDB2m

Essential Oils & Aromatherapy

http://amzn.to/1ouuZTx

Superfoods that Kickstart Your Weight Loss

http://amzn.to/1eyHdku

The Best Secrets Of Natural Remedies

http://amzn.to/1gmHd7y

The Hypothyroidism Handbook

http://amzn.to/1emWfyR

The Hyperthyroidism Handbook

Essential Oils Box Set #19: Body Butters for Beginners & Soap Making for Beginners

http://amzn.to/1kqLQCp

Essential Oils & Weight Loss For Beginners

http://amzn.to/Q83bFp

Top Essential Oil Recipes

http://amzn.to/1lSrhSC

Soap Making For Beginners

http://amzn.to/1fkmYwr

Body Butters For Beginners

http://amzn.to/1fWjwJe

Apple Cider Vinegar For Beginners

http://amzn.to/1joDzX2

Homemade Body Scrubs & Masks For Beginners

http://amzn.to/1jjLRIO

Essential Oils Box Set #1 (Weight Loss + Essential Oil Recipes

http://amzn.to/1qlYWWP

Essential Oils Box Set #2 (Weight Loss + Essential Oil & Aromatherapy

http://amzn.to/1qlYWWP

Essential Oils Box Set #3 Coconut Oil + Apple Cider Vinegar

Essential Oils Box Set #19: Body Butters for Beginners & Soap Making for Beginners

http://amzn.to/1oIFZJw

Essential Oils Box Set #4 Body Butters & Top Essential Oil Recipes

http://amzn.to/1jSxURJ

Essential Oils Box Set #5 Soap Making & Homemade Body Scrubs

http://amzn.to/RAvJYo

Essential Oils Box Set #6 Body Butters & Body Scrubs

http://amzn.to/RAvSel

Essential Oils Box Set #7 Top Essential Oils & Best Kept Secrets Of Natural Remedies

http://amzn.to/1gvsRCq

Essential Oils Box Set #11 Carrier Oils for Beginners & Coconut Oil for Easy Weight Loss

http://amzn.to/1nHfy6X

Essential Oils Box Set #12 Essential Oils Weight Loss & Essential Oils Aromatherapy & Natural Homemade Cleaning Supplies & Top Essential Oil Recipes & Carrier Oils
http://amzn.to/1nHfy6X

Essential Oils Box Set #13 Superfoods & Essential Weight Loss & Essential Aromatherapy & Body Butters & Soap Making
http://amzn.to/1nUds6v

Essential Oils Box Set #14 Weight Loss & Apple Cider Vinegar & Body Butters & Homemade Body Scrubs & Coconut Oil for Beginners
http://amzn.to/1i1qYOd

If the links do not work, for whatever reason, you can simply search for these titles on the Amazon website to find them.

Lightning Source UK Ltd.
Milton Keynes UK
UKOW06f2112270317
297645UK00011BA/149/P